Little Lambs
# Peter the Fisherman

by Karen Williamson
Illustrated by Sarah Conner

CANDLE
BOOKS

Peter was a fisherman.
He and his brother Andrew
had a little fishing boat.

Each day they went fishing on Lake Galilee.

One day Jesus came to the lake.
"Please let me get into your boat," he said.

Crowds of people were listening from the shore.

Standing in Peter's boat, Jesus told them some of his wonderful stories.

When he had finished, Jesus said,
"Peter, sail into deep water and let
down your nets. We're going fishing!"

"It's no use," said Peter.
"We fished all night – and caught nothing."

"But, Jesus, if you want me to," said Peter, "I'll try again."

So Peter and Andrew sailed out on the lake,
where the water was deep.

They let down their net.
When they tried to pull it up,
it was so full of fish it started to tear!

The fishermen landed their
huge catch of fish.
"Now come with me," Jesus said.
"I've got special work for you to do."

At once they dropped their nets
and followed Jesus.

Another time, Peter was in a boat
with Jesus and his other friends.

All of a sudden,
a big storm came up.

Waves tossed the boat
from side to side.

Jesus' friends felt
very scared.

But Jesus was lying fast asleep in the boat.

They woke Jesus.

"Help us," they shouted.
"We're all about
to drown!"

Jesus stood up.
"Be quiet," he told the wind.
"Be still!"

At once the storm stopped.
Everything was calm again.

"It's amazing!" said Peter and his friends.
"Even the wind and the waves obey Jesus!"

Peter was one of Jesus' closest friends.